Unless As Stone Is

Unless As Stone Is

Sam Lohmann

Variations from Dante's sestina beginning
Al poco giorno e al gran cerchio d'ombra

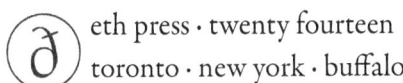

eth press · twenty fourteen
toronto · new york · buffalo

UNLESS AS STONE IS
© 2008 Sam Lohmann

This work is licensed under a Creative Commons Attribution-NonCommercial 4.0 International License. To view a copy of this license, visit: http://creativecommons.org/licenses/by-nc/4.0/ or send a letter to Creative Commons, 444 Castro Street, Suite 900, Mountain View, California, 94041, USA.

First published in 2008 by "The Firm and Aerie", Portland, Oregon.

This edition published in 2014 by
eth press
an imprint of punctum books, Brooklyn, New York
ethpress.com | punctumbooks.com

eth press is a parascholarly poetry press interested in publishing innovative poetry that is inspired by, adapted from, or otherwise inhabited by medieval texts.

eth press is an imprint of punctum books, an open-access and print-on-demand independent publisher dedicated to radically creative modes of intellectual inquiry and writing across a whimsical para-humanities assemblage.

David Hadbawnik, Chris Piuma, and Dan Remein are the editors of eth press, and we can be contacted at ethpress [at] gmail.com. We are currently accepting proposals and submissions.

ISBN-10: 0615983928
ISBN-13: 978-0615983929

Library of Congress Cataloging-in-Publication Data is available from the Library of Congress.

Cover art: *Arm/Frog* by Michaela Curtis-Joyce.
Cover and book design by Chris Piuma.

1

By a knoll or a wall or under green
leaves we have seen them dressed in green

shape they would of shaken stone

with such love we bore their shadows
even this match won't catch that

spry green, the faithless hills piaffe

even the river swerves, runs back to the
small day and its tidal shadow.

An infinite thirst drinks infinitely.
You have a crush on Persephone.

As ions aspire, grass sought up a stone:
we stole our final resting place.
Hell yes, I whisper to myself—

as a man whispers *Hide!* in the grass.
His science has progressed past stone.

Some Golden Rules I thought of last night.

Hiss, scient asp or greased piston;

as sign's hasp or grist turns to regress,
past's tone is grasped;

as ions aspire, grass sought up a stone,
a sighing sass, poor grace to pass on:

siren's purr grates diapason

on stone in grass. Wake up,
undo a locked chest.

So it turns out: buried treasure
you've come running to escape:
nimble, perturbed, they turned and hilled
out your flat shadow.

A vanishing act is involved in every
such story, and bundled grass

and buried treasure. Such story is
a fast wind you have come running.

2

Some Golden Rules I thought of last night:

When a woman wakes up, a stone
stays in the grass, a rooted shadow.

...And, brushing sleep out of roomy eyes,
I see a narrow shadow light
on the day's things, and rise.

I sleep on stone, go around eating grass
to see: crisp yellow and green she twines.

The funny grass, lares of hills,
and her edgewise shadow. Stone leers

where hills ossify, seasons scatter,
and faithless green garbles the lady
who prisons grass in her land-poor shadow.

She walks the hills, nudging shadow
aside, of a sudden, edaphic woman
flickering now as stone, as grass.

Perch, easy mischief, crisp yellow
a lover'd see: vie out a vestigial verity,

pose an arbor herbal, choose
a fugitive peony, percolate perpetual
scamper at a coat-tail, be sole
pervader, leave any star all umbrage, aim us
erratic in trapeze, peal forte,

in eldritch tempo belch amor.

3

Is the crown of grass
or the green dress
necessary?
You splice the colors

so exactingly, out of their shadows

Eros glares
hard as lime
that locks stone.

We are not moved or are moved like stone,
by the honey-slow reason
that thaws the hills and turns them—say
anon come aperture,
eldritch tempo, cherries!
It turns the mind because it mixes
crisp yellow and green—cold and calling,
copper of florets, itchily fought, coinvaded.

As a mind hides a stone ingress
where a snake snakes where a hollow hollows,

you find killdeer eggs hidden in the open
in a crown of dirt and twined grass;

a ways away—nimble, perturbed, enamored,
never undiverted, perpetual scamper—

I fake a broken wing. See
fate arch elaborate mess, impenetrable.

4

So I fly over plains and hills
to escape, lasso a shadow, swipe
at any penumbra, pause in dolor,
undo a locked chest,
or wander, perturbed, enamored.

The hills go pale and their whole shadow
—as someone hides a day among days—
hides me, stone, grass, anything.

The tall day under the sickle's shadow
glints—tiny copper of florets,
olive and amber. Punier
as the day returns, hills pale, and she's
gone or a shade—some Golden Rules
you thought of last night. Wake up, undo—

(Calcined stone shatters, free!)

(You have a crush on Persephone.)

Through the spiral day
a newel shadow,

and in the phototonic grass
an indecent shadow; elsewhere
I saw the thin day eating fat shadow;
elsewhere,

greener than grass, she makes a stone
shiver, quickens a glacier.

Because you said, *These are my hills
now, those are my mountains, I'm*

well rounded, our shadows took a sharp curve,
flickered at strangers' faces

and here, and there—fey hills
pelted with nitty-gritty grass

to garble the eye—

at the small of day—

5

From white to green because you mingle
crisp yellow and green so

Eros who locks us as in amber
leers from shadows where

he is frozen snow, not moved, unless
as stone is that hears
the season turn; and when
it speaks, he disappears.

As a man hides in grass, a stone's
turned back, and again I have run
the numbers to evade this grass
shadow this woman wall this green
whenever peers from the shade a woman
pares a man parts. Whenever
a woman goes as a man grazes

her science has progress past stone.

Go to the lady don't come back.

Shadow the lady. Go to grass
don't come back. Man the factories. Woman
the facts. Go to the shadow don't
come back. Capture the town's
thin outline, color it fat:

Go to the window tell the wind.
It won't come back.

6

*Flesh green and hair green
green how I want you green—*
coppered like he wants me, calcined,

stoned, ladied, shadowed, hilled
into the grass, as a man
hides a woman hides a stone clasp

on a sash of shadow meadow shadow
show how much I lady.

Green, how can she want him
green unless as stone is
stone, how can he want me
unless as cloud as woman,
unless as man as shadow, how
can eye undress endless unless

unless a hill turn, a woman close
the day in her book on shadow?

But, coming to in Arcady's crosshairs
as the day falters, see
how grass fingers sought up the stone
to seize name and date. When a shadow

aches to be the crooked stem
I thought up all night, it only slinks
away by a knoll or wall or under;

when the bough breaks, a leaf lifts.

7

By plain and hill to such a wall
we see her green—a spired stone—
bear his very shadow; so

we wish air rounded by high May rivers,
or soft green wood catch fire as fair
for her sake: so we sleep her life
a shade makes disappear

mid air—a man in grass.

They eat of shadow, whiten from the grass,
and their desire won't change, root stone
that speaks and hears a woman:

She arms the hills and makes May
cover them with flowers and ants.
She has a grassland on her mind.
She mingles waving lovely wise
that comes to shadow.

Some Golden Rules I thought of last night
catch fire every morning. Others wait—
lynxes low in the grass:

where the day bends, the shadow leaps
great arcs it can't explain.

Here where the hills drooled shadow—this
clutch of treasure spilt in the grass
at X. Others leap and catch.

All our oddity operates
on changing verity: The rivers
may turn and run uphill
or a green branch catch fire

as shadows marinate green and yellow
to twine, turn our mind: See
fate arch elaborate mess: Wake up,
undo a locked chest.

Unless As Stone Is was written in spring and summer 2006, when I was attending the Evergreen State College and working as a wetland conservation intern for the Washington State Department of Transportation. Revision occurred in fits over the next two years, continuing a conversation with Dante's sestina as I read and reread it somewhere between original and translation (I don't know Italian). Chance operations informed the writing at various points but did not constrain it. I used phrases from George Kay's prose translation in *The Penguin Book of Italian Verse* and from my own semantic and homophonic elaborations. Other phrases were taken from Loren Eiseley ("His science has progressed past stone"), Federico García Lorca ("Flesh green and hair green..."), Sappho ("greener than grass"), Michaela Curtis-Joyce ("You have a crush on Persephone" and "These are my hills..."), and a wetland biologist named Fred ("Some Golden Rules I thought of last night"). I am grateful to all of the above for the working materials.

Thanks are due also to Chris Piuma and eth press for so generously giving the poem this new form; to Portland's Independent Publishing Resource Center (where I initially self-published this poem, in an edition of about 70); to Michaela again, for the cover image, and again for everything.

Dante's sestina may be read online at
http://www.ethpress.com/dante

www.ingramcontent.com/pod-product-compliance
Lightning Source LLC
Chambersburg PA
CBHW070850160426
43192CB00012B/2386